The Wisdom of
Old-Time Television

The Wisdom of
Old-Time Television

Common Sense and Uncommon Genius
From the Golden Age of Television

Compiled and Edited by Criswell Freeman

WALNUT GROVE PRESS
Nashville, TN
(615) 256-8584

ISBN 1-887655-64-6

The ideas expressed in this book are not, in all cases, exact quotations, as some have been edited for clarity and brevity. In all cases, the author has attempted to maintain the speaker's original intent. In some cases, material for this book was obtained from secondary sources, primarily print media. While every effort was made to ensure the accuracy of these sources, the accuracy cannot be guaranteed. For additions, deletions, corrections or clarifications in future editions of this text, please write WALNUT GROVE PRESS.

Printed in the United States of America
Cover Design by Mary Mazer
Typesetting & Page Layout by Sue Gerdes
Edited by Alan Ross and Angela Beasley
1 2 3 4 5 6 7 8 9 10 • 96 97 98 99 00 01

ACKNOWLEDGMENTS
The author gratefully acknowledges the helpful support of Angela Beasley, Dick and Mary Freeman, Mary Susan Freeman, and Tom Gerdes. The author also extends heartfelt appreciation to Captain Kangaroo for his encouragement during the formative years of this project.

For Mary Jo and Donna

My Dearest Old-Time TV Pals

Table of Contents

Introduction

In 1948, Texaco moved its popular *Star Theatre* from radio to a new and unproven medium which produced tiny black-and-white images on a blurred cathode-ray tube. Thus began the golden age of television.

During those early years, reception was poor, equipment was unreliable, and shows were by today's standards — primitive. Despite these drawbacks, television first captured then dominated the national imagination.

Half a century has passed since Uncle Miltie and Howdy Doody were fresh faces on the small screen, but an important legacy remains. Generations of Americans grew up with stars like Lucy, Desi, Jackie and Red. Thankfully, we haven't forgotten these old friends.

This book chronicles the genius and humor of our favorite old-time television personalities. Because they succeeded against long odds, these men and women have earned the right to share their insights on the human condition And, because we've come to know them so well, their words have special meaning.

Eve Arden, a.k.a. Our Miss Brooks, once wrote, "Life is made up of so many memorable moments, and while I'm not one to live in the past, there are certain 'jewels' I enjoy dribbling through my fingers." The following jew els of wisdom come straight from the men and women who created television land. Sit back, relax, and take a brief trip down memory lane. And, whatever you do, don't touch that dial

1

Television

Early television was visual Vaudeville. The most popular programs featured dancers, singers, animal trainers, jugglers and comedians. Variety shows filled the small screen with non-stop action.

Ted Mack's Original Amateur Hour was the first radio show to make the transition to television. Over the next decade, others followed, and dramatic radio programming withered. TV became America's primary source of entertainment. Here's what the stars had to say about it.

In 1947, virtually everything the industry
knew about television, radio taught us.
Buffalo Bob Smith

Television is great.
I hardly ever watch radio anymore.
Gracie Allen

Television has ten times the impact of radio.
Jack Webb

I consider the television set
   as the American fireplace, around which
      the whole family will gather.

Red Skelton

Television is the medium
      of the 20th century.

Hugh Downs

We shall stand or fall by television.

E. B. White

Television is the only way
I know to entertain
20 million people
at one time.

Imogene Coca

Television is the quickest form of recognition in the world.

Lucille Ball

I have a great respect for TV.
I'm not one of those actors who looks on it
as slumming. You get a wonderful chance to
develop the character — something you
can't have in movies or the theatre.

Raymond Massey

Saying you don't like television is like
being stranded in the middle of the ocean and
saying you don't like water.

Darren McGavin

The audience is never wrong.

Carol Burnett

I cry all the way to the bank.

Liberace

We live in a big and marvelously varied world.
Television ought to reflect that.

Edwin Newman

The faultless formulas of television —
the ones that last — are simple.

Dick Clark

Imitation is the sincerest form of television.

Mighty Mouse

Television has proved that people
will look at anything rather than each other.
Ann Landers

Advertising is the greatest art form
of the 20th century.
Marshall McLuhan

There's not enough music on television.
Mitch Miller

Television is like
indoor plumbing.
It didn't change people's
habits — it just kept them
inside the house.

Alfred Hitchcock

In the early days of television,
        what you saw was what you got.
        We did not have a second chance.

Milton Berle

The TV racket is too tough.
        I like movies better.

Frank Sinatra

Television is tough work,
        but I'm not giving up. After all,
        you can't quit when you're 39.

Jack Benny

2

Life

Television has not always mirrored life's harsh realities. In its Golden Age, TV was pure entertainment. It was a medium of escape not introspection. A 1954 edition of *TV Guide* observed, "Life is just one mad whirl for the Roller Derby crowd." So much for deep thoughts about the human condition.

Even if their characters kept things on the lighter side, old-time television celebrities did think deeper thoughts. On the following pages, stars share their ideas about the most fascinating dramatic presentation of all: life.

Whether we're prepared or not, life has
a habit of thrusting situations upon us.

Lucille Ball

Like the seasons of the year,
life changes frequently and drastically.
You enjoy it or endure it as it comes and goes,
as it ebbs and flows.

Burgess Meredith

It happens to be a fact as one gets older,
one does get wiser. It's simply
the way the calendar crumbles.

Rod Serling

Life offers what it will, and thinking about it
too much is not helpful.

Orson Bean

My greatest weakness was that I spent
too much time thinking about Garry Moore.

Garry Moore

Hope for the best.
Expect the worst.
Life is a play.
We're unrehearsed.

Mel Brooks

Life is available
to anyone no matter
what age. All you
have to do is grab it.

Art Carney

All acts have a beginning and an end.

Edgar Bergen

Do you know how important now is?
Enjoy it as much as you can, because
no matter how much you want to hold
on to "now," it's going to be "was."

Sid Caesar

The real fear is not death —
it is the fear of wasting life.

Jackie Gleason

You've got to recognize that
there will never be another you.

Mickey Rooney

In life, all good things come hard,
    but wisdom is the hardest to come by.

Lucille Ball

We all have a purpose in life.
I don't think anyone's purpose is any greater
    than anyone else's. My purpose is
        to make people laugh.

Red Skelton

Most crises disappear as weeks
    and months go by. The perspective of time
        is nature's own sweet song.

Efrem Zimbalist, Jr.

Life has so much fun in it. Look for
    the comic relief, and you can't be unhappy
        for long.

Carl Reiner

It's up to each of us to contribute something to this sad and wonderful world.

Eve Arden

The power of a young imagination
    is important in shaping a life and
        in shaping the world itself.

Adam West

The days in my life that stand out most
vividly are the days I've learned something.
Learning is so exciting I get goose bumps.

Lucille Ball

I prefer to live on a year-to-year basis.
Life is exciting if you keep making it exciting.

Steve Allen

It's nice to be successful,
     but nice isn't the essence of living.
          Struggle is.

Mary Tyler Moore

Life isn't about arriving someplace.
     If you're moving, that's the most
          you can ask for.

Richard Chamberlain

I want to be a lively old lady.
     When I'm 80 years old I want my kids
          calling me saying, "Why don't you
               ever call any more?"

Carol Burnett

Everything in this whole business is timing.
I don't just mean timing your performance —
life is timing, too.

Art Carney

The problem is to fashion one's existence,
which is difficult because so many people
want to fashion it for you.

Jack Palance

You know what my biggest luxury is?
Being able to use time as I see fit.

Merv Griffin

What we should ask of ourselves is growth,
not perfection.

Pat Boone

Life does not have to be
perfect to be wonderful.

Annette Funicello

We are all
cremated equal.

Jane Ace

3

Happiness

Many years ago, *New Yorker* magazine featured a cartoon summing up television's concept of happiness: A middle-class couple sat watching TV. The woman turned to the man and said, "I'll make a deal with you. I'll try to be more like Harriet if you try to be a little more like Ozzie."

Unfortunately, true happiness requires something more than a good Ozzie Nelson imitation. How much more? Stay tuned to find out.

I think there will always be a place
for a wholesome, happy approach to life.

Ozzie Nelson

Then it hit me —
being unhappy was something I'd been *doing*,
and when I stopped doing it, I reverted to
my natural state, which is happy.

Orson Bean

Never indulge in jealousy or envy.
Those two destructive emotions
will eat you alive.

Loretta Young

Nothing will kill you quicker
than unhappiness.

Phyllis Diller

I've never really had too many worries.
If that's bland, then I'm bland —
and glad of it.

Perry Como

Contentment is a perishable commodity.
That's what makes it so precious.

Burgess Meredith

Do your daydreaming in the daytime so that
your mind is free to sleep at night.

Dave Garroway

The perfect day? If you wake up and you
aren't in the obituaries, it's a good start.

Johnny Carson

I keep learning that the secret of being happy
is doing things for other people.

Dick Gregory

Feeling useful to others
is a very important part of happiness.

Dennis Weaver

I love my work, but work itself
doesn't add up to happiness.
Happiness is sharing a life.

Michael Landon

Even if the show's successful,
it doesn't mean I'm going to live
happily ever after.

Andy Griffith

Happiness is having a large, caring, close-knit family in another city.

George Burns

Happiness

The good things happened to me almost
by accident, usually when I wasn't looking.
Danny Thomas

Stay busy and take care of
your own business.
Eddy Arnold

As long as I can work, I'm happy.
Lucille Ball

Happiness means having something to do
and something to live for.
Bishop Fulton J. Sheen

I'm convinced that if there were
more old-fashioned front-porch swings,
there would be more happy marriages.
Walter Cronkite

Don't go looking for happiness. Happiness is a by-product.

Johnny Carson

When puppies overeat, they refuse to play.
People are like puppies. They play best
when they're a little hungry.

Jane Wyman

People who lack purpose
are unhappy people.

Jackie Gleason

Nobody is completely happy.
I don't look for perfection anymore.
Right now is perfection.

Sid Caesar

Other people are like a mirror that reflects
back on us the kind of image we cast.

Bishop Fulton J. Sheen

You can't find happiness
by trying to take it
from another person.

Dawn Wells

It takes a little time to figure out that you
can't do everything, nor are you equipped to.
That's not laziness — it's maturity.

Dick Clark

I've learned you're no happier in big houses
than you are in modest ones.

Michael Landon

The root of all disease is fear. Fear of what?
Fear of yourself. Become unafraid of yourself,
and you lose your fear of other things.

Robert Young

Success, we must remember,
is in the eye of the beholder.

Tennessee Ernie Ford

Happiness to me means constant growth.

Eddie Albert

Happiness is a matter
of your own doing.
You can be happy
or you can be unhappy.
It's just according to the
way you look at things.

Walt Disney

4

All-Purpose Advice

In 1950, a red-haired comedienne named Lucille Ball faced a major career decision. Lucy starred in a popular radio show, while her husband, Desi, was a successful band leader. Now they were about to risk everything in television, and Lucy was worried. Would the show succeed? Was this a wise career move? What if she flopped?

One night, a dear friend appeared to Lucy in a dream. Carole Lombard, a comic actress who had been killed years before in a plane crash, came to Lucy with sound advice. Lombard's words were short and sweet: "Honey, go ahead. Take a chance. Give it a whirl."

Lucy awoke with a firm resolve to move forward with her new television show, and, as it turned out, Lombard was right: we *did* love Lucy.

Old-time television stars share their thoughts on a wide range of topics. Follow these words to the letter, unless, of course, you can dream up better advice on your own.

Try and live your life the way you wish other people would live theirs.

Raymond Burr

Things happen in their own good time.
So don't fight life, but go with it
one step at a time.

Donna Douglas

Learn from your mistakes.
Don't beat your head
against the same mistakes.

Lucille Ball

Better to trust a man
who is frequently in error than
one who is never in doubt.

Eric Sevareid

Don't worry. Be happy. Feel good.
Aphorism on Larry Hagman's bathroom mirror

A human being's first responsibility
    is to shake hands with himself.

Henry Winkler

If you're not yourself,
    you eventually hate yourself.

Roger Smith

The secret to happiness is being yourself.
I'm me and I like being me real good.

Dan Blocker

Love yourself first.

Lucille Ball

Whats the secret of enjoying old age?
        I can't tell you. It's a secret.
                                    George Burns

The secret to staying young
        is to live honestly, eat slowly,
              and lie about your age.
                                    Lucille Ball

Don't retire.

                                    George Burns

Age is a case of mind over matter.
        If you don't mind, it doesn't matter.
                                    Jack Benny

If you find a dull place,
it's generally not
the fault of the place.

Ed McMahon

Here's my advice about money —
make it. Money buys lots of things
including more money.

George Burns

Everyone should make two fortunes —
one to blow and one for old age.

Jackie Gleason

Don't lend money.

Eddy Arnold

The greatest waste of money is to keep it.

Jackie Gleason

An ounce of prevention
is worth a pound of bandages.

Groucho Marx

Nothing seems impossible to kids.

Allen Funt

Don't offer advice to your kids
until they ask for it.

Ozzie Nelson

The best advice of all may be no advice.
That's not my line.
It's from a fortune cookie.

George Burns

To unwind, there's
nothing like an oboe and
a glass of nice, warm milk.

Mitch Miller

5

Adversity

Looking back on his many ups and downs, Walt Disney said, "You may not realize it when it happens, but a kick in the teeth can be the best thing in the world for you." One actor discovered Disney's words to be true — literally.

Walter Brennan lost his front teeth in a movie accident. As a result, Mr. Brennan began playing old men, finally garnering the role of Grandpappy Amos in *The Real McCoys*. Brennan claimed, "The luckiest thing that ever happened to me was a kick in the face!"

If you've been "kicked" — consider the quotations that follow. And remember that your greatest roles may be just around the corner.

As a child, we were so poor that
my family's menu consisted of two choices:
take it or leave it.

Buddy Hackett

How to survive tragedy?
Throw yourself into work, work, work.

Raymond Burr

Struggle is wonderful. Failure is fabulous.
Poverty is the greatest wealth-maker of all.

Julie Newmar

Hardships are wonderful for us.
They make us strong.

Lawrence Welk

Before I became successful,
   I flopped plenty. It was a rocky road,
      but I never quit going out on stage.

Milton Berle

Throughout life, failure snaps at our heels
like a great mongrel dog. The key to success
      is realizing that the dog is really
            a harmless puppy.

Jackie Gleason

Learn to laugh at yourself,
   and you'll find yourself laughing at things
      that would make other people cry.

Sid Caesar

I'm older now and I've faced crisis
    many times. I have found over the years,
        if I am quiet and patient, it will pass.

Burgess Meredith

Pain nourishes courage.
    You can't be brave if you've only had
        wonderful things happen to you.

Mary Tyler Moore

Character is not revealed
        when life shows its best side
        but when it shows its worst.

Bishop Fulton J. Sheen

Some tragedies you never get over.
But part of life is living with our losses
and going on.

Buffalo Bob Smith

The past was either good or bad. Either way,
you can't change it. Why relive it over and
over again? The only thing you can change
is your future.

Jackie Gleason

The cure for fear?
A little more faith.

Rod Serling

The tougher the fight,
the more important
mental attitude is.

Michael Landon

6

Success

In the world of television, success is a two-edged sword. Notable roles often lead to a dreaded theatrical malady: typecasting. Dwayne Hickman will forever be Dobie Gillis. Tina Louis will remain the glamorous Ginger of Gilligan's Island. We remember Barbara Eden as Genie, Elizabeth Montgomery as Samantha, and Jerry Mathers as the Beaver.

Adam West gained white-hot fame as Batman but spent years in the shadows after the show was cancelled. West looked at his situation philosophically, saying simply, "No two careers run the same course."

Each of us must take a different path to success. Thankfully, the journey, while uniquely our own, is not without guideposts. For good directions, stay tuned.

Success is a long climb up a slippery rope.

Audrey Meadows

You don't sit down and deliberately write a classic. You just do the best you can and hope for success.

Walt Disney

You can have success if you can handle it.

Donna Douglas

Anytime anybody tells me the trend is such and such, I do the opposite. I got where I am by coming off the wall.

Clint Eastwood

If you want to make it, you've got to have a pretty good opinion of yourself.

Jackie Gleason

Success

It's my first conviction that an actor
   must be a businessman. His business is
a self-contained one. It is, in fact, himself.

Hugh O'Brien

A beautiful face gets you the first five minutes.
   After that, you're on your own.

Loretta Young

You've got to be lucky,
      but then you've got to be able
      to take advantage of the luck.

Chuck Connors

You have to be at the right place
      at the right time. But then you
      have to be ready.

Johnny Carson

Everything worthwhile, everything of any value, has a price. The price is effort.

Loretta Young

Success

You can't be what you aren't.

Dorothy Collins

I would rather be a failure in something
that I love than be a success
in something I hate.

George Burns

If you want a formula for failure, it is this:
Ignore the public.

Lawrence Welk

Get a good idea and stay with it,
and work it until it's done and done right.

Walt Disney

I don't want to set the world on fire.
I just want to keep warm.

Ernest Borgnine

Success wasn't due to any genius on my part.
I've always been able to surround myself
with good people. Nobody is *that* right
without good people.

Jack Benny

If you don't know what you're doing,
you're likely to be afraid of the wrong things
and be careless of the real dangers.

Hugh Downs

When you have instant success,
you can't help wondering if
it could end just that fast.

Bob Newhart

First, you must believe you can do it.
Then do it. That's success.

Mother's Advice to Pat Boone

The rat race to see who has the biggest
house or the most expensive car is pointless.

Hugh O'Brien

You don't have to be a rotten rat
to get ahead in show business.

Carol Burnett

It isn't the rat race unless you run with rats.

Perry Mason

Success has nothing
to do with what you
gain in life or accomplish
for yourself. It's what
you do for others.

Danny Thomas

Success requires teamwork. There's no such thing as a good Amos and a bad Andy.

Joe Garagiola

7

Love

In 1960, CBS introduced us to the world of a small-town sheriff named Andy Taylor. The warmth and honesty of his village, a mythical place called Mayberry, was experienced on both sides of the lens.

Andy Griffith recalled, "That show was special. Here was a group of people who could all work together with no ego problems. Nobody cared who got the joke or who came up with it."

Today, *The Andy Griffith Show* is firmly established as a national treasure. The exploits of Andy, Barney, Gomer and Opie continue to entertain millions of fans. How does one explain this popularity? Clever writing, certainly; wonderful characters and talented actors, of course. Of equal importance is the sense of caring that pervades every episode. Let's call it love — Mayberry style.

The wise person
understands that his own
happiness must include
the happiness of others.

Dennis Weaver

My important goals have to do with my family,
not my Nielson ratings.

Michael Landon

I've often thought it would be wonderful
to be a *femme fatale*, but I wouldn't trade that
for what I've had: a family, and real love.

Eve Arden

There is a rare beauty that comes from the soul.
Beauty comes from within.

Eva Gabor

A career, no matter how successful,
is meaningless unless someone you care
about is able to share that success with you.

Martin Landau

You have to answer to yourself first,
and, when your cup is full, the love
can be given to someone else.

Dawn Wells

Insanity is hereditary —
you get it from your children.

Sam Levenson

To love children is to love God.

Roy Rogers

Love the public the way
you love your mother.

Maurice Chevalier

Either you master your emotions
or they master you. Uncontrolled love
can burn you out.

Loretta Young

The surest way to a woman's heart
is to be interested in what she's thinking.

Tina Louise

If you can't stand yourself, neither can anybody else.

Sid Caesar

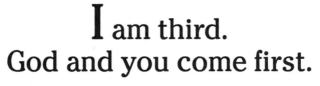

I am third.
God and you come first.
Sign in Danny Thomas' Office

8

Attitude

TV actors learn quickly the benefits of a positive attitude. Before landing that first important role, an actor's life is a series of try-outs and rejections. Then, once stardom is attained, ratings must be maintained. For each series that becomes a classic, fifty are cancelled and forgotten.

Amid these challenges — and possibly because of them — television's legendary performers offer valuable advice about attitude. Bob Newhart once said, "All I can say about life is this: Enjoy it." Same to you, fella.

My greatest asset is the capacity to dream.

Merv Griffin

If you can dream it, you can do it.

Walt Disney

We're all dreamers.
We have to dream about what we want
before we can get it.

Lloyd Bridges

The most common ailment of all men — the strange and perverse disinclination to believe in a miracle.

Rod Serling

Attitude

If you have a negative thought,
don't waste hours thinking about it.
Simply direct yourself to something positive
and keep repeating the positive until
you eliminate the negative.

Tina Louise

Attitude is the most important thing
in comedy.

Joey Bishop

The hardest thing you will ever do
is trust yourself.

Barbara Walters

The only talent I had was a big mouth
and a reputation as a baseball comedian.
Oh yes, and I had one other thing:
I considered myself the greatest
undiscovered actor in the country.

Chuck Connors

It doesn't do any good to put yourself down.
If other people are going to have negative
thoughts, that's their problem.

Carol Burnett

It was my mother's belief — and mine —
to resist any negative thinking.

Audrey Meadows

Self-pity is
the great masochistic tranquilizer.

Jackie Gleason

Acting, or anything else,
    is simply a matter of controlling
      your mind and body.

Lorne Greene

Don't pay attention to the critics,
    because they disagree. Listen to that
      still, small voice of your own.

Burgess Meredith

When we line up all the facts
    that we believe are against us, those facts
    can stop us before we start. The facts,
      after all, speak for themselves —
        except they're not true.

Marlo Thomas

Each of us makes his own weather.

Bishop Fulton J. Sheen

Think about what's coming,
        not about what went.

Jackie Gleason

I keep looking ahead because I'm a reporter.
    A reporter is always concerned
        with tomorrow.

Edward R. Murrow

The mind is like a clock that is constantly
    running down. It has to be wound up
        daily with good thoughts.

Bishop Fulton J. Sheen

An optimistic mind is a healthy mind.

Loretta Young

Life is a game show where the people who enjoy it are the winners.

Orson Bean

Always be in a state of becoming.

Walt Disney

9

Kindness

Early on, an important figure emerged in television land: the wise father. These men could be stern and tough, but underneath their rough exteriors, they were softies. Robert Young played such a character in *Father Knows Best.* Andy Taylor was another perceptive pop. So was Danny Williams in *Make Room for Daddy*.

On the short list of great TV dads is Ward Cleaver, father of Wally and The Beave. Played by Hugh Beaumont, Ward was sometimes hotheaded. But, with a little help from June, he always discovered right from wrong by the end of the show.

In one memorable scene, father Ward gave Theodore a simple lesson on kindness: "Son, there are people who trample on others. You beat them by never becoming like them."

Gee, Dad — you're swell!

Morality is how you behave toward people.
Julie Newmar

I've always said
   it doesn't cost any more to be nice.
Soupy Sales

The less secure a man is, the more likely
   he is to have extreme prejudices.
Clint Eastwood

It doesn't hurt to be nice to people.
   Besides, that's what the public wants.
Lawrence Welk

Nobody rides alone.
It's the code of the West.

Andy Devine

If you must wake someone up, do it with good cheer.

Dave Garroway

If a man is stingy, he's stingy all his life.

Jack Benny

Never mistake kindness for weakness.

Red Skelton

Respect is a two-way transaction,
    but it begins at home with self-respect.

Eric Sevareid

There is one thing I would like
    on my headstone: a line that reads only,
        "He left friends."

Rod Serling

Charm is simply this:
the golden rule,
good manners, good
grooming, good humor,
good sense, good habits,
and a good outlook.

Loretta Young

Judge your neighbor
by his best moments,
not his worst.

Bishop Fulton J. Sheen

Friendship, like a good
television show, is built
on mutual honesty.

Arthur Godfrey

10

Work

Milton Berle once complained, "My brother ought to try to get a job so he'll know what kind of work he's out of." In a later response, Steve Allen poked fun at Uncle Miltie, observing, "Berle's ad libs aren't worth the paper they're written on."

In truth, both Allen and Berle shared something more than comedic genius. Both learned about work the hard way: by being television stars.

Television was and is a grueling profession. The hours are long, the work is unforgiving, and the pressures are intense. Ozzie Nelson, a man who never seemed to have a job on television, was, in real life, a hard-working director, producer and actor. Each year, the Nelson family completed 39 episodes in as many weeks. Still, the imperturbable Ozzie was not overly concerned: "We don't worry about all 39 shows each season. We just do one at a time, and they all get done in due course." Just as we thought: Nothing phases Ozzie.

The world doesn't owe you a living.
Nothing is more important than being able
to stand on your own two feet.

Lucille Ball

Getting anywhere in one's lifetime
is the result of self-discipline, of work —
and I mean hard work.

Loretta Young

Luck is hard work and realizing what
opportunity is — and what it isn't.

Lucille Ball

Be decent and fair.
But ultimately you have to know how
to get the work done, whether or not
people like you for it.

Sally Field

My best advice: Fall in love with what you do for a living.

George Burns

There's no labor
a man can do that's
undignified — if he
does it right.

Bill Cosby

What's wrong with children today
is mental unemployment.

Jackie Gleason

Do you want to be successful?
Nurture your talent.

Tennessee Ernie Ford

I'm a firm believer that anything
you get for nothing loses value.

Larry Hagman

You can't do good work if you're only
going through the motions. You've got
to enjoy what you're doing.

Ricky Nelson

Work hard and go home happy.

Michael Landon

Work

The great green god Money; I hate it.
I'm not pursuing money, it's pursuing me.

Danny Thomas

I'd rather make $200 a week doing something
I love than a million dollars doing
something I hate.

George Burns

Two hours of desk work tires me more
than eight hours with the band.

Lawrence Welk

Approach everything realistically and
give it the best caring effort you know how.

Andy Griffith

The only reason to retire is if you can find
something you enjoy more than what you're
doing now. I guess I've been retired
all my life.

George Burns

The Wisdom of Old-Time Television

I'm always on the side of action.
I can't just sit on my butt
and do *Green Acres.*

Eddie Albert

The only way you'll know that something
is going to get done is to do it *now.*

Sid Caesar

Discussion is the most excellent means
to avoid decision.

Bishop Fulton J. Sheen

People find gold in fields, veins, river beds
and pockets. But wherever you find gold,
it takes work to get it out.

Art Linkletter

All our dreams can come true —
if we have the courage to pursue them.

Walt Disney

Difficulty is the excuse
history never accepts.

Edwin Murrow

I work 80 hours a week. I play the game hard,
but it's worth it.

Ed Sullivan

I know I'm working too hard when my kids
stop calling me Daddy and start calling me
Tennessee Ernie.

Tennessee Ernie Ford

Work hard? You gotta'. You can't goof off.
Only unemployed actors sleep late.

Gene Barry

Hard work surpasses natural talent.

Dwayne Hickman

If you want to kill time,
try working it
to death.

Sam Levenson

Learn to take your work seriously and
not yourself seriously.

Clint Eastwood

Retirement? Never!
That would kill me faster than a heart attack.

Liberace

I don't like looking back. I'm looking ahead
to the next show. It's how I keep young.

Jack Benny

11

The Performance

The best performances become so real that art doesn't just imitate life, it recreates it. Young Tony Dow was cast as brother Wally on *Leave it to Beaver*, but his mother was worried. She feared the role might rob Tony of a normal childhood. He pleaded for a chance to take the part: "It isn't really acting, Mom. It's swimming and playing and climbing and stuff."

Barbara Hale spent years as the dutiful Della Street on *Perry Mason*. One of Barbara's small children was asked what mom did for a living. The youngster replied, "She's a secretary."

Most of us will never see our names roll across the credits of a hit television show, but we are still performers on the stage of life. The following insights will help reality become art.

That camera is like a telescope.
   If you're phoney, it shows up right away.
The only way you make it in this business —
   or any other — is by being natural.

Ed McMahon

You must approach an audience with the
   right attitude. When you do, they know it.
   You can't fool an audience.

Art Linkletter

Know yourself — and know your audience.

Tennessee Ernie Ford

I'm trying to sell every audience something.
   That something is me.

Eddy Arnold

If you have timing and an understanding
of people, and if you don't get too
stage-frightened, you'll be all right.

Buddy Ebsen

When I'm not trying to impress the audience
or the critics, my acting is wonderful.

Orson Bean

As I look back 35 years ago,
I think my performance could have been better
if I hadn't worried so much
about the performance.

Milton Berle

In acting, be natural.
Effort kills the performance.

Roger Smith

Never give up on an audience.

Red Skelton

A late-night TV show should never be heard.
It should be overheard.

Joey Bishop

What I like best is not performing for an
audience but communicating with them.

Shari Lewis

Acting is a way to overcome
your own inhibitions. The writer creates
a strong, confident personality,
and that's what you become —
unfortunately only for the moment.

Shirley Booth

I've never been jealous of another performer.
There's room for every single person
in the world.

Sheri Lewis

I never forget that I'm in somebody's house,
and I behave as though I'm a guest.

Jackie Gleason

I always act like a guest in the house.
I wouldn't dream of throwing anyone
a curved question.

Edward R. Murrow

If we're having fun,
the audience is having fun.

Red Skelton

Nothing is expensive
if it shows up on the screen.

Ozzie Nelson's Favorite Quotation from Cecil B. DeMille

An actor, if he is lucky,
may get three great parts in a lifetime.

Lee J. Cobb

Acting is simple.
I just do what they tell me to do.

James Arness

I loved playing Lucy Ricardo.
I got to act out all my childhood fantasies.

Lucille Ball

It's so important to have what I call
the enchanted sense of play.

Lucille Ball

The secret to
our appeal is simple:
Mother likes our music.

Lawrence Welk

12

Comedy

Turn-of-the-century poet Ella Wheeler Wilcox wrote, "Laugh and the world laughs with you, frown and you frown alone." Great comedians occupy a special place in our hearts because comic genius is always in short supply.

Old-time television was home to many great comics; some, like *The Three Stooges*, were masters of slapstick; others, like Jack Benny, relied on impeccable timing. Still others relied on rapid-fire one-liners, à la Henny Youngman.

On the following pages, we learn the secrets of comedy from a few past masters. These men and women made the world laugh. And we're still smiling.

A clown is a warrior who fights gloom.
Red Skelton

A comedian is a man who can stand up and be funny whether he says anything or not.
Buddy Ebsen

A comic says funny things.
A comedian says things funny.
Ed Wynn

Absolute terror is the clown's secret.
Terror that they won't laugh.
Red Skeleton

Comedy is truth. You take truth and
   you put a little curlicue on the end.

Sid Caesar

I don't deal in jokes. I deal in reality.

Jonathan Winters

Getting into trouble and getting out of it
   will always be the essence of comedy.

Lucille Ball

Comedy is tragedy revisited.

Phyllis Diller

Tragedy + Time = Comedy

Steve Allen

Comedy never changes. There are only
eight or nine formats of jokes. If it sounds like
a new joke, it's been taken from someplace.

Milton Berle

Jokes are like folklore, difficult to define, with
an origin buried in a multiplicity of sources.
Just remember, nothing that's funny
is ever new! Or vice versa!

Milton Berle

We tried to amuse ourselves.
We didn't make cartoons for children.
We didn't make them for adults.
We made them for ourselves.

Mel Blanc

There's nothing funnier
than the human animal.

Walt Disney

To me, a healthy belly laugh is one of the most beautiful sounds in the world.

Bennett Cerf

You can't hate other people when you're laughing with them.

Eddie "Rochester" Anderson

13

The Stars

Adam West was granted an audience with Pope Paul VI. Upon meeting the Caped Crusader, the Pontiff happily proclaimed, "I love your show Mr. West. Your costume is very striking."

West, surprised by his newly discovered fan, responded, "Yes, your excellency, though not as striking as your own."

Pope Paul, ever the courteous host, replied, "But *your* automobile is more impressive than mine!"

The moral of this story? It's no bat-surprise: TV stars are bigger than life, even to a Pope.

The Stars

I'm the straight man.
I set 'em up and Gracie knocks them down.
It's a very nice family arrangement.

George Burns

Liberace is TV's first real matinee idol.

Chicago Tribune, 1954

Red Skelton is the most unacclaimed clown
in show business. He's the logical successor
to Chaplin.

Groucho Marx

Milton Berle is the greatest comic
around here.

Red Skelton

Milton Berle is responsible
for selling millions of TV sets.
I sold mine, my uncle sold his....

Joe E. Lewis

Buddy Ebsen is the guy
who never met a man who didn't like him.

Fess Parker

Fred MacMurray is as down-to-earth
as applesauce.

Hedda Hopper

Jackie Gleason was a vibrant character
of a thousand lights and colors.

Audrey Meadows

Wholesome?
Ozzie and Harriet could have played
old Salem in the days of Cotton Mather.

Cleveland Amory

Beaver was played with fetching naturalness by little Jerry Mathers.

Variety, 1957

Music changes, but I don't.

Lawrence Welk

I have an agreement with Lawrence Welk.
He laughs at my jokes,
and I laugh at his music.

Henny Youngman

Dick Van Dyke is just right
    for good, fun family shows.

Walt Disney

Whenever asked about my best effort
of all the things I've done in show business,
    I answer unhesitatingly,
    The Dick Van Dyke Show.

Carl Reiner

Saying how I feel about the *Van Dyke Show*
    is like saying how I feel about my family.

Mary Tyler Moore

Raymond Burr was
    a warm, friendly, compassionate man
    whose heart was as big as his body.

Barbara Hale

Perry Mason dominated my life.

Raymond Burr

I'm the only guy in the world who ever
turned the oboe into a commercial asset.

Mitch Miller

Give *Gunsmoke* all you've got and
you'll be a big star.

John Wayne

His Advice to James Arness Who Had Originally
Turned Down the Role of Matt Dillon

*B*ewitched is not about cleaning house.
It's about a very different relationship,
and I think people pick up on that.

Elizabeth Montgomery

Some comedians are tight inside,
but Andy Griffith is *warm*.

Don Knotts

The Jack Benny we see on-stage is like
a member of your own family. There's a
thirty-year build-up to every punch line.

Don Wilson

The Stars

Carson is a master of the cozy pace
and mood that be believes are appropriate
for the muzzy midnight hours.

Time Magazine, 1967

For years I've been Johnny Carson's idol.
Then, all of a sudden, the whole thing
switched, and Johnny Carson became my idol.
Do you want to know something?
It's not nearly as much fun this way.

Jack Benny

When people ask me,
"Aren't you Chet Huntley?" I answer, "Yes."
Actually, it's the polite answer, because really
it doesn't make any difference.

David Brinkley

Good night, Chet.
Good night, David.

David Brinkley, Chet Huntley
Sign-off Lines on the Final Huntley Brinkley Report, July 30, 1970

The Wisdom of Old-Time Television

I guess I'm a star, but I don't figure
Rawhide will last forever.

Clint Eastwood

Ed Sullivan will be around
as long as someone else has talent.

Fred Allen

I never had the ambition to be something.
I had the ambition to do something.

Walter Cronkite

Most of my fans watched as children and
grew up with *Gilligan's Island*. I've found
that being a good childhood memory
is very rewarding.

Bob Denver

Remember me with smiles and laughter
for that is how I will remember you all.
If you can only remember me with tears,
then don't remember me at all.

Michael Landon

Even on a flickering, pallid TV screen,
Lucille Ball's wide-set, saucer eyes beam
with the massed candle power
of a lighthouse on a dark night.

Time Magazine, 1952

I tried to provide hope, faith and fun.

Lucille Ball

14

Observations on Easy Payments, Middle Age and Other Facts of Life

We conclude with a potpourri of thoughts on a wide range of topics. Enjoy.

Observations

For civilization to survive,
civilization has to remain civilized.

Rod Serling

I believe the world will either destroy itself
or settle things by law.

Raymond Burr

The excuse for our existence is still the same
as it ever was: to serve our Creator
by serving our kind.

Arthur Godfrey

Politics is the art of looking for trouble,
finding it everywhere, diagnosing it incorrectly
and applying the wrong remedy.

Groucho Marx

This used to be a government
of checks and balances. Now it's
all checks and no balances.

Gracie Allen

It's too bad that all
the people who know how
to run the government are
busy driving taxicabs
and cutting hair.

George Burns

Spend time with your parents. They're not around forever.

Hugh O'Brien

There's nothing wrong with being a little unreasonable when you think you are right.

Richard Boone

Glamour is only the attention-getter.
It never brings us the things
we want most of all.

Loretta Young

Never doubt that a woman makes up
her own mind — even if she's only five.

Allen Funt

I hate housework!
You make the beds, you do the dishes —
and six months later you have
to start all over again!

Joan Rivers

Cleaning your house while your kids
are still growing is like shoveling the walk
before it stops snowing.

Phyllis Diller

Proverbs help us all be better Mouseketeers.

Jimmie Dodd

Any time you want to
wipe out hard luck, just
use work as the eraser.

Pat Boone

If you listen to your conscience, it will serve you as no other friend you'll ever know.

Loretta Young

There's only one way to learn anything,
and that's to stand on your own feet
and do it.

Hugh O'Brien

The major ingredient of any recipe for fear
is fear of the unknown.

Rod Serling

It's worse to spend yourself
on profitless emotions than it is to spend
hard-earned money on valueless trifles.

Loretta Young

One of the most
interesting things in life
is mastering something
that you haven't
yet mastered.

Barbara Feldon

Ⓞne of the greatest wits
of all times was
the person who
called them
"Easy Payments."

George Burns

Diets are for those who are thick
and tired of it.

Mary Tyler Moore

A race track is a place
where windows clean people.

Danny Thomas

A hospital bed is a parked taxi
with the meter running.

Groucho Marx

There's not a thing wrong with television
that not watching it won't cure.

Franklin P. Jones

Immigration is the sincerest form of flattery.

Jack Paar

Once you're a character on a TV series,
you're that character for life.

Carol Burnett

Middle age is when you're faced
with two temptations, and you choose the
one that gets you home by nine o'clock.

Ronald Reagan

You know you might
be getting old when
your favorite section
in the newspaper is
50 Years Ago Today.

George Burns

The very best advice is to be a good listener
and think before you talk. People who talk
before they think get into hot water and
are very sorry later.

Mickey Rooney

There's nothing complicated
about what you do with a promise.
You make it. You keep it.

Loretta Young

Good manners are nothing more than
the practical application of the Golden Rule.

Loretta Young

I love the sound of real live people laughing
at what they enjoy.

Carol Burnett

No one can deny you need some money
to create happiness. But the oldest tag line
in the world is so true:
Money isn't everything.

Lucille Ball

A truly charming person never has time
for envy, self-pity or gossip.

Loretta Young

A family ought to be a lot more
than a collection of mutual needs.
It ought to be fun.

Art Linkletter

What is success? It's not five million dollars.
It's your contentment and your family's.

Frank Fontaine

Miss Kitty would drift out of Dodge if it weren't for Matt Dillon.

Amanda Blake

If I can't take it with me, I won't go.

Jack Benny

Good-bye, kids.

Clarabell

Sources

About the Author

Criswell Freeman is a Doctor of Clinical Psychology living in Nashville, Tennessee. He is the author of *When Life Throws You a Curveball, Hit It* and *The Wisdom Series* from WALNUT GROVE PRESS. He is also a published country music songwriter.

About Wisdom Books

Wisdom Books chronicle memorable quotations in an easy-to-read style. Written by Criswell Freeman, this series provides inspiring, thoughtful and humorous messages from entertainers, athletes, scientists, politicians, clerics, writers and renegades. Each title focuses on a particular region or special interest.

Combining his passion for quotations with extensive training in psychology, Dr. Freeman revisits timeless themes such as perseverance, courage, love, forgiveness and faith.

"Quotations help us remember the simple yet profound truths that give life perspective and meaning," notes Freeman. "When it comes to life's most important lessons, we can all use gentle reminders."

The Wisdom Series
by Dr. Criswell Freeman

Wisdom Made In America
ISBN 1-887655-07-7

The Book of Southern Wisdom
ISBN 0-9640955-3-X

The Wisdom of the Midwest
ISBN 1-887655-17-4

The Book of Texas Wisdom
ISBN 0-9640955-8-0

The Book of Florida Wisdom
ISBN 0-9640955-9-9

The Book of California Wisdom
ISBN 1-887655-14-X

The Book of New England Wisdom
ISBN 1-887655-15-8

The Book of New York Wisdom
ISBN 1-887655-16-6

The Book of Country Music Wisdom
ISBN 0-9640955-1-3

The Wisdom of Old-Time Television
ISBN 1-887655-64-6

The Golfer's Book of Wisdom
ISBN 0-9640955-6-4

The Wisdom of Southern Football
ISBN 0-9640955-7-2

The Book of Stock Car Wisdom
ISBN 1-887655-12-3

The Wisdom of Old-Time Baseball
ISBN 1-887655-13-1

The Book of Football Wisdom
ISBN 1-887655-18-2

Wisdom Books are available through booksellers everywhere.
For information about a retailer near you, call 1-800-256-8584.